When Boys and Girls Become Men and Women

When Boys and Girls Become Men and Women

Everything You Need to Know about Growing Up

Written by
Jörg Müller

Illustrated by
Dagmar Geisler

Translated by
Andrea Jones Berasaluce

Sky Pony Press
New York

Sky Pony Press books may be purchased in bulk at special discounts for sales promotion, corporate gifts, fund-raising, or educational purposes. Special editions can also be created to specifications. For details, contact the Special Sales Department, Sky Pony Press, 307 West 36th Street, 11th Floor, New York, NY 10018 or info@skyhorsepublishing.com.
Sky Pony® is a registered trademark of Skyhorse Publishing, Inc.®, a Delaware corporation.
Visit our website at www.skyponypress.com.

10 9 8 7 6 5 4 3 2 1

Manufactured in China, December 2019
This product conforms to CPSIA 2008

Library of Congress Cataloging-in-Publication Data is available on file.

Cover provided by Loewe Verlag GmbH
Cover illustration by Dagmar Geisler

Print ISBN: 978-1-5107-4656-5
Ebook ISBN: 978-1-5107-4667-1

Table of Contents

For Your Parents

Kids have many questions and always want to know everything. Sometimes this isn't so easy for parents. Especially if their children aren't little boys and girls anymore so much as young men and women. That's why we've created this book. It should accompany kids and parents on the long road to becoming adults. We want to help both sides explore this new territory step by step.

The Small Difference

It's Good That Everybody Looks Different

There's a well-known Swedish fable about a race between a hare and a hedgehog. The clever, prickly fellow with short legs won the race because his wife looked identical to him. And the hare never noticed that there were two hedgehogs. But that only happens in folktales. In real life, it is very rare that two people look so alike as to be confused for one another.

The difference between a man and a woman can almost always be identified immediately. That's what we'll focus on for the next few pages—along with the differences you can't see immediately because they are hidden under pants, sweaters, and dresses.

Each Has Its Strengths

Sometimes you hear a lot of nonsense when it comes to differences between boys and girls or men and women. For example, it's often claimed that boys are strong and girls are weak. Or they say that one gender is dumb and the other is clever. What's interesting is how these silly prejudices came about.

Let's take the prejudice of intelligence and stupidity. Historically, it was almost entirely sons that went to school or learned a profession in order to earn money and support a family of their own. The daughters often received no vocational training at all. They learned to make handicrafts or to play a musical instrument. If they worked, it was at most as a nanny or a factory worker.

"You'll be married soon anyway. Then you'll have children and must keep the house. Why then should we pay for an expensive education?" many parents thought at the time.

Today it is very different: Girls have the same opportunities as boys if they want to study or learn a trade. And anyone can see that girls are at least as smart as boys. You only have to look at their grades in school.

Even when boys say that girls are physically weaker, that is not entirely true.

Although men are usually stronger, taller, and heavier, women, however, are often more tenacious and have more endurance.

Additionally, men are much more sensitive to pain than women. A man, for example, might not withstand childbirth. As such, each gender has its strengths . . . .

We're strongest together.

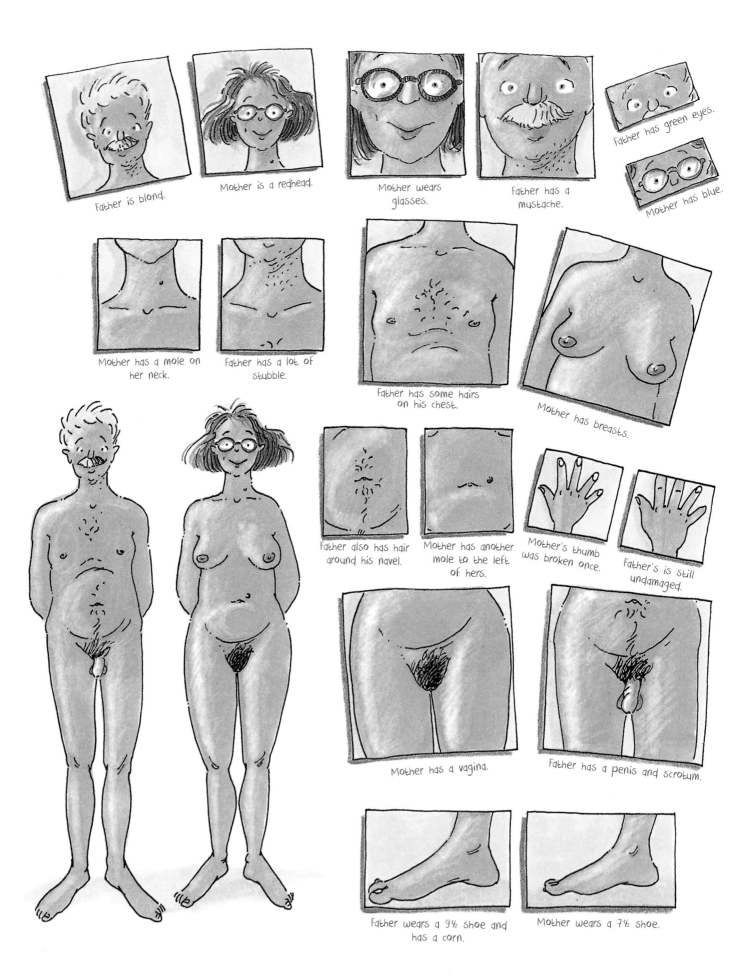

Father is blond.

Mother is a redhead.

Mother wears glasses.

Father has a mustache.

Father has green eyes.

Mother has blue.

Mother has a mole on her neck.

Father has a lot of stubble.

Father has some hairs on his chest.

Mother has breasts.

Father also has hair around his navel.

Mother has another mole to the left of hers.

Mother's thumb was broken once.

Father's is still undamaged.

Mother has a vagina.

Father has a penis and scrotum.

Father wears a 9½ shoe and has a corn.

Mother wears a 7½ shoe.

Let's Take a Closer Look

One thing that really is different in men and women will only stand out when each one is naked: Between the legs, there are very clear differences!

Boys and men have a scrotum hanging there, which looks like a small pouch, and in front hangs the **penis**.

Girls and women have an opening between the legs called the **vagina**. They have nothing hanging between their legs. Yet women and older girls have on their upper body something men lack: **breasts**.

When someone has something that you yourself do not, it is an exciting thing. But: How can one figure out the secret behind these differences? Many children try to discover it for themselves along the way, especially if they enjoy to frequently disrobe while at home.

Of course, parents mostly aren't too thrilled when everyone is hopping around the room naked.

So what good is it if you can see what's different but not know why? There's so much happening inside the bodies of boys and girls that you can't see; inside there are many more interesting differences.

Sure, I'm a frog, but they look naked as jaybirds to me.

What Girls Want to Know About Boys

What's Hanging There Between the Legs?

Hanging between their legs, men and boys have a scrotum and a penis. The tip of the penis is called the **glans**. The long part is called the shaft.

There are no bones in the penis. It consists only of skin, blood vessels, erectile tissue, muscle fibers, and nerves. The blood vessels are tiny, flexible tubes through which blood flows. They are surrounded by muscle fibers and form the erectile tissue. There are three parts of the penis shaft.

One is the urethra. It runs like a small hose through the penis shaft into a man's lower abdomen. There it flows into the bladder, where fluid from food and beverages accumulates. This fluid is called urine. When a boy goes to the bathroom, urine runs out of the penis through the urethra.

The end of the urethra can be found in a small hole in the glans. To urinate it is necessary to pull back the foreskin, which covers the glans, to the shaft.

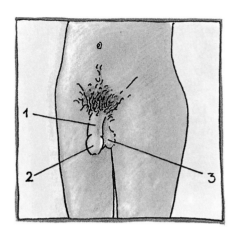

1 Penis shaft
2 Glans
3 Scrotum

Some parents have their sons' foreskins removed. It is not so incredibly important for the body. Then the washing of the glans is easier because it is exposed.

The glans is the most sensitive part of the man's body, and its skin is very smooth. Under its surface, especially at the bottom edge where the foreskin begins, it is studded with nerve endings. These nerves function like small power lines. They report every touch of the glans immediately to the brain.

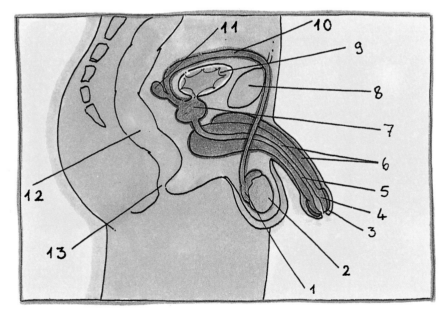

1 Epididymis
2 Testicle
3 Foreskin
4 Glans
5 Urethra
6 Erectile tissue
7 Prostate
8 Pubic bone
9 Urinary bladder
10 Vas deferens
11 Seminal vesicles
12 Bowel/intestine
13 Anus

The Penis Can Change

If the glans is gently touched, often when a man or a boy is very excited, the erectile tissue fills with blood. The penis becomes bigger. When the erectile tissue is full of blood, it feels really hard. Almost as if there were a bone inside.

This moment in which the penis is very stiff is called an erection. It can be double the size it is in its normal state. And the foreskin pulls back by itself. You can also see the color of the glans has changed. It is darker, because the excess blood shimmers through the skin. When the erection subsides, the blood flows back out of the erectile tissue. The penis becomes softer and smaller again.

How Semen Gets Produced

The urethra doesn't only transport urine. Semen is also transported out of the body through it. Semen is used in order to form a baby by fertilizing the woman's egg cell. We'll explain that in more detail later.

Inside the scrotum, there are two chambers. In each of these, there is a testicle. From the outside, one can feel the testicles, or testes. They feel like small balls and have a slightly oval shape, similar to an egg. The left testicle is normally larger and lies a bit lower than the right.

Semen is produced in the testes. The finished semen is then collected in the epididymis, of which there are two. They are like thin egg-cups set over the testes and are also found in the scrotum.

1 Testicle
2 Epididymis
3 Prostate
4 Urinary bladder
5 Vas deferens
6 Seminal vesicles
7 Urethra
8 Erectile tissue

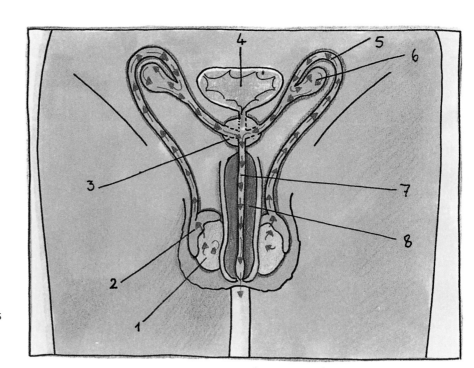

From each of the two epididymises flows a **vas deferens** like a small hose to the **seminal vesicles**. Within them the thick semen is thinned out, so it can later flow much more easily through the urethra.

The point where the vas deferens flow into the urethra is called the **prostate**. This is where the semen is further diluted. The prostate works like a valve. It prevents urine and semen from mixing. It only allows semen to flow through the urethra when the penis is stiff.

When the stiff penis is stimulated even more, for example by stroking the glans, it results in an **ejaculation**. During an ejaculation, the seminal fluid from the prostate is conducted through the urethra and sprayed out of the body through the penis.

What then comes out in a milky-white fluid is called **sperm**. It is only the smallest part of the semen. Most of the liquid is formed in the prostate and seminal vesicles. The liquid is designed to ensure that the sperm can be quickly sprayed through the urethra.

The Scrotum is a Small Marvel

If you look at the scrotum you can see that it is darker than rest of the skin on the body. In addition, it often looks a bit wrinkled. The skin contains a lot of sweat glands and sebaceous glands. Therefore it can be very rough and bumpy. The scrotum forms the cover and protection for the testicles. This protection is necessary because the testicles are very sensitive to pressure and impact. An accidental bump, when playing soccer for instance, can induce hellish pain.

The temperature in the testes must remain the same in order for sperm cells to be made. Above all, the testicles should not become too warm. That's why they hang in a pouch out-

side of the body, which is three degrees cooler. And so that the testicles do not get too cold, there is a built-in automatic system. At very low temperatures, the muscles in the scrotum draw together. This moves the testicles closer to the warm body, protecting them from the cold. Every boy can observe this himself when he goes swimming in very cold water.

What Boys Want to Know About Girls

Most Things are Hidden Within the Body

Most of the unique features of girls and women aren't visible at a glance because they're hidden within the body. However, there is one particular feature that can often be used to immediately recognize adult women: the **breasts**.

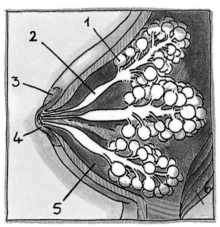

1 Lobules
2 Mammary glands
3 Areola
4 Nipple
5 Adipose tissue
6 Muscle

Their size and shape are different for every woman. The breasts are composed of connective tissue, fat, and glands. On the breasts are the nipples. Underneath these are mammary glands, the output of which flows to the nipples. For a woman who has a baby, these glands produce breast milk, which the infant suckles from the nipples.

There are many nerve ends in the nipples. This is why the skin on the nipples is very sensitive.

The rest of women's genitals are much deeper inside than in men. If you run your hand from the navel down, you can feel the mons pubis. In grown women, this is where curly pubic hair grows. Right below the mons pubis are the outer labia. These are two folds of skin. They touch like two protective hands, covering the other, even more sensitive parts of the woman that can only be seen if the outer labia are somewhat separated. Underneath are the inner labia. Because they are crisscrossed by many blood vessels, they're dark pink in color.

Where Girls and Women Have Their Most Sensitive Spot

A little below the mons pubis, in just the spot where the inner labia begin, lies the **clitoris**. It is also often called the clit. The clit, which feels like an ingrown pea under the skin is, for nearly all women, the most sensitive part of the body—similar to the glans at the end of the penis. Like under the skin of the glans, the clit also has many, many nerve endings. These immediately report every instance of contact to the brain.

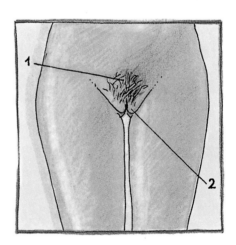

1 Mons pubis
2 Outer labia

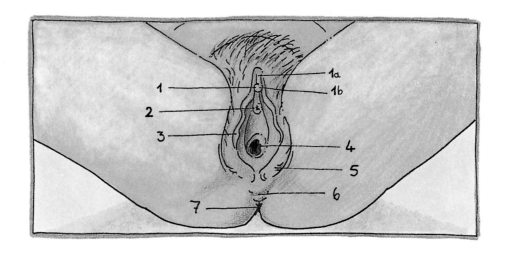

1   Clitoris
1a Shaft
1b Tip
2   Urethra
3   Inner labia
4   Vagina
5   Outer labia
6   Perineum
7   Anus

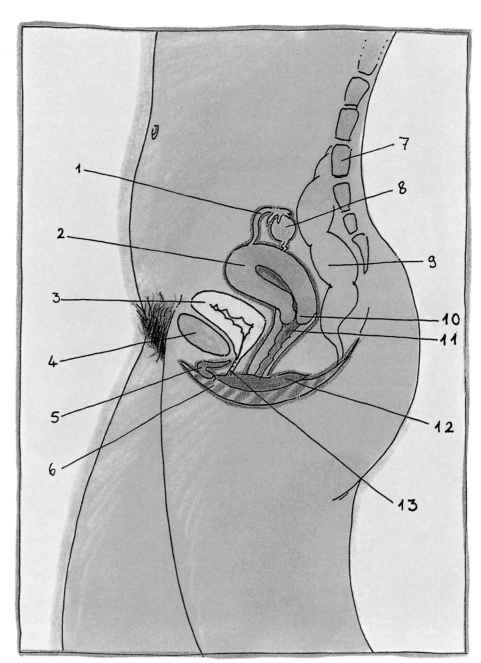

1   Fallopian tube
2   Uterus
3   Urinary bladder
4   Pubic bone
5   Clitoris
6   Outer labia
7   Spine
8   Ovary
9   Bowel/intestine
10 Cervix
11 Vagina
12 Inner labia
13 Urethra

A woman's clitoris and a man's glans have even more in common. Just as when a man's penis is touched, it stiffens and enlarges, the clitoris too can grow larger. When the skin around either is stroked, for example, they both can almost double in size. Then they are much more sensitive than before.

Under the clitoris there is a small opening: This is a woman's **urethral opening**. Now it's clear why girls don't pee standing up like boys: Their urethra cannot be controlled with the hand. However, perhaps boys should also sit to pee because even the most practiced sometimes miss the target.

Below the urethra, there is another opening: the vagina. In young girls, it is often closed off by a thin membrane. In this membrane, called the **hymen**, there is a small hole. It looks different for every girl. For example, if a girl does a lot of sports, the opening in the hymen can be bigger than in other girls.

What We Cannot See from the Outside

The rest of a woman's sexual organs cannot be seen from the outside because they are inside the body.

Right behind the hymen is the vagina. You can think of it as consisting of muscle fibers, like tubes up to ten centimeters long. On the inside wall are countless small glands. If the outer genitals are caressed, these mucous membranes in the vagina secrete a fluid, which moistens the inner vaginal wall.

At the top end of the vagina is the **cervix**, which connects to the **uterus**. The uterus looks quite similar to a pear with its thinner part pointing downwards and is also about the same size. Located within the abdomen, it is approximately in the middle, between the navel and beginning of the **labia**.

The uterus consists of a thick layer of muscle. These muscles are unbelievably stretchy. You can almost imagine the uterus like a balloon which has not been inflated. The reason it must be stretchy because it was designed to make room for a baby.

Emerging from upper part of the uterus are the **fallopian tubes**. They look like two small hoses whose upper ends expand like funnels. These funnels end at the **ovaries**, which lie to the right and left of the uterus, one on each side.

When a girl is born, her ovaries already contain about four hundred thousand prepared eggs. But only a few hundred will become ripe in a woman's lifetime and thus available for **fertilization** by male sperm. An egg becomes ready for fertilization through an exciting process that takes place in a woman's body over the course of about twenty-eight days. This process, which is constantly repeated, is called the **menstrual cycle**.

1. EGG MATURATION

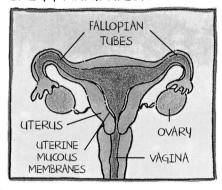

2. OVULATION

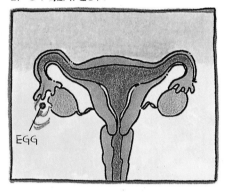

3. LUTEAL PHASE

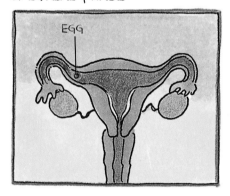

4. MENSTRUATION

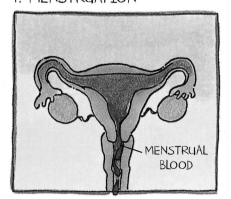

The Menstrual Cycle

Each cycle begins with one of the many **egg cells** maturing in the ovaries and becoming ready for fertilization. A finished egg cell is still so tiny that you can't see with the naked eye.

It takes fourteen days, more or less the entire first half of the cycle, until the egg cell is ripe. Then it jumps from the ovary into the fallopian tube's funnel. This is called **ovulation**.

The egg needs four days in order to move through the fallopian tube to the uterus. There, a thick mucous membrane has now formed on the uterus.

About fourteen days after ovulation, the body forms a new mucous membrane in the uterus. Together with the dead egg, it is secreted from the body. A mixture of blood and mucus then flows out of the vagina. This is **menstruation**.

Often this bleeding is referred to as a **period**, as it comes on a regular basis. Many women also speak about their "time of the month." This is quite logical to explain because the bleeding lasts for about four to six days. But a woman does not lose as much blood as one might think. On average, it is about four small shot glasses full of fluid, at least half of which is mucus.

Many women feel a tug in their abdomens on their periods. Sometimes this can even really hurt. That is due the muscles in the uterus contracting in order to better get rid of the egg, blood, and mucus.

Girls and Boys Grow Up

When Does It Begin?

"Wait until you grow up…!"—girls and boys hear this all the time. But when is someone really grown up? When do you finally become an adult?

Growing up begins with puberty, which for most boys starts at about twelve years old, while girls it's often on their tenth birthdays. The body then slowly starts to change. On the following pages we will explain in detail what happens with everything in the body during this lively time.

When the changes begin is different for everyone. Although we could say at what age the majority do something, there will be one kid for whom puberty comes sooner and another later. It is therefore quite normal that there will be differences for you and friends of the same age.

You can talk with them at length about what happens in puberty. You will mostly know just as much as each other. Often friends tell each other half-truths, because they don't want to admit that they have no way to know.

If something unusual comes up, it's better to ask your parents, though it tends to be just the time when it isn't so easy to get along well with them. They don't realize right away that their children are now becoming adults. But many boys and girls don't want to be treated like little children by parents or teachers. Therefore, it's not uncommon to quarrel.

In order not to have a stressful relationship with your parents, you should have a lot of patience during this time. They have—just like you—to first learn that you are becoming an adult.

What Happens to Boys' Bodies

Usually the first changes in boys begin between the tenth and twelfth year of life. At eighteen, puberty and growth are almost always fully completed.

Everything starts with the testicles and the scrotum growing. About a year later the penis also becomes larger.

When the testicles and penis grow, **hormones** are produced in the testes. These can be thought of as a tiny little letters that swim around in the body. Through them, the testicles tell all the body parts that the boy should now become a man. So the bones find out that they are supposed to grow, and quickly. Therefore, when boys start puberty, most tend to grow quite fast.

At the base of the penis and around the scrotum grow the first pubic hairs, and soon after, hair grows in the armpits.

Finally, mostly around the fifteenth birthday, the first mustache hairs sprout over the upper lip. The hormones let the larynx become larger in the neck. The vocal cords in the larynx become longer and the voice changes: it becomes deeper and rougher and sounds much more masculine. While the vocal chords grow, it can sound very strange at first. Sometimes the voice is hoarse or sounds a bit like Mickey Mouse. That's what people mean when they say a boy's voice is breaking.

In the upper part of the body, the hormones let the nipples grow somewhat. Sometimes there is swelling around the nipples. That can hurt, but it is quite normal and usually goes away by itself.

"Wet Dreams"

The hormones can also really annoy a boy: During puberty it happens often that the penis suddenly becomes erect for no reason. Sometimes you might wake up in the morning with an erect penis. This is not unusual, and it is typical for the penis to become smaller again after a few moments. In addition, spontaneous erections become increasingly rare towards the end of puberty.

With the onset of puberty the production of sperm starts in the testes. Every day new sperm cells grow there and collect in the epididymis. But at some point there are too many. The body needs to get rid of them and does so quite automatically. A boy then is not alone in experiencing ejaculation at night. His first "wet dreams" he can get sometime between his 13th and 15th birthday. He could now even father children.

What Happens to Girls' Bodies

For most girls, puberty begins two years earlier than for boys. First a girl notices that her nipples are changing: they grow bigger and become more prominent. This often happens around the tenth birthday.

In the following years, the breasts begin to form. But it is very slow; the development often takes up until her seventeeth or eighteenth birthday. During this time, it often happens that the breasts look different from each other. This can be because the breasts change until they are "grown." There are also adult women with one breast larger than the other.

In the first stage of breast development, girls often feel a tightness in their breasts. Sometimes the nipples are very sensitive.

Rubbing against clothes can chafe and hurt. It is best then to wear a bra and to pad the nipples with a bit of cotton/stuffing.

At the same time when the breast starts to change, a girl's sex organs begin to grow. The uterus and the ovaries and also the labia become larger. And similar to in the testes of boys, there are now hormones produced in girls' ovaries that go all over the body in order to promote growing up. There is a growth spurt, just like for boys.

As the breasts begin to develop, girls grow their first pubic hairs on the mons pubis. A little later, the first underarm hairs appear. By age seventeen, it is not uncommon for a girl's pubic hair to look like that of an adult woman.

About two years after the start of puberty, one of the most exciting developments for girls occurs. The body prepares for its monthly cycle and first **menstruation**. The mucous membranes in the uterus form a transparent, whitish fluid, which flows out of the vagina. That's called **vaginal discharge**.

Many girls are alarmed by vaginal discharge. But there is no reason for this. Only if the fluid has a very unpleasant smell, or is dark in color, or if the labia feel an itchy or burning sensation, should you go to the doctor. Six to twelve months after a girl's first vaginal discharge, her first period comes.

Everyone is the Same—and Yet Everyone is Different

When the body changes during puberty, it is an exciting thing. And everyone is curious as to whether the same things are happening to their friends and classmates.

The girls might take note, in the swimming pool, for example, whose breasts are growing. And the boys might compare each other's penis sizes.

Some of the girls talk about other girls, and how they have very large breasts. And some boys are awfully proud that their penis is much larger than others'. But that may change. Some girls develop later or more slowly than other girls. And some boys will overemphasize the importance of penis length.

Although it's good to be proud of your body, becoming a grown up depends on many other things unrelated to physical attributes—for example, being smart, kind, and understanding. Those are qualities to strive for.

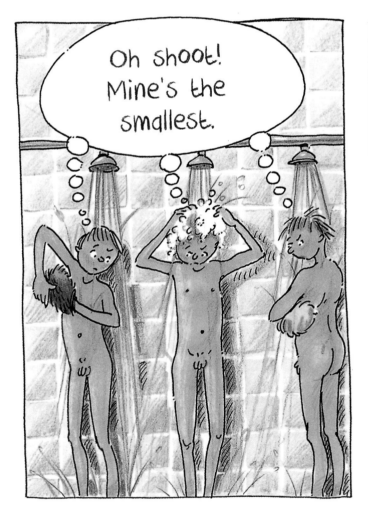

Nobody Likes to Talk about This

It's quite normal to be curious. That's why it is good and important for children to get to know their own bodies. One way for them to do this is to touch themselves. This very natural act is a special experience for every girl and boy; it can feel good to touch your own genitals.

Perhaps you have already tried playing with your genitals. When you do and feel pleasure—so much that you may not want to stop—it is called **masturbation**.

Adults also caress their genitals in order to experience such feelings. It's just that we barely talk about it! Unfortunately, some adults claim that masturbation is obscene. Often these adults will say all sorts of nonsense to make kids afraid to touch themselves. However, statements like "masturbation makes you sick and stupid" are lies.

Furthermore, rumors such as "it causes pimples" or "it will make your genitals stop growing" are only meant to scare you. Masturbation is a completely natural need that everyone has.

Good Personal Hygiene

Many Teens Have Skin Problems

What's particularly unpleasant about puberty for many boys and girls is that the skin goes haywire. Far too much skin oil builds up in the sebaceous glands. You can see this in how the skin, especially on the face, begins to glisten. The extra oil can clog your sebaceous glands, or pores. When these clogged pores form a small black dot, they are called **blackheads**. Sometimes these become inflamed and from the blackheads, thick red **pimples** form, which are filled with pus. Doctors call this skin condition **acne**. Unfortunately, the worst part is where the pimples are: on the face, back, and shoulders.

You should never squeeze pimples. They often go away by themselves. If you remove them by force, you can get scars that never go away.

If the acne is very bad or has not improved by the end of puberty, **dermatologists** and **gynecologists** can help.

When boys or girls suffer from acne, people say sometimes that they have bad skin. But this just means that they naturally have a lot of blackheads and pimples and might need extra help with skincare. It doesn't mean that they don't wash their skin enough. On the contrary: Too much washing with normal soap is bad for the skin. It can cause even more pimples. The best thing to do when you have acne is to get a special skin cleanser recommendation from a dermatologist.

A MORNING IN EIGHTH GRADE . . .

LOVE STORY

After a week of waiting, Charlie got his wish: He had a date with Sabine.

Not Too Little and Not Too Much

Sometimes you get lucky and your parents don't notice that you just made a few faces in front of the bathroom mirror and totally "forgot" to wash up in the evening. However, during puberty you should wash particularly thoroughly. Your skin produces more grease and sweat, which can cause skin blemishes and body odor.

Now that you're becoming an adult, the areas under your arms and between your legs need regular washing!

However, don't make the mistake of washing your genitals with a lot of soap. It destroys the skin's natural protective acid mantle, or barrier. Even when you experience itching or burning, don't use soap. On the contrary: It irritates the skin even more and makes everything worse.

It is better to simply use lukewarm water and a mild cleanser to wash yourself. If you do this twice a day, there's no need to use soap on your genitals.

Especially for Boys

The penis and scrotum should be washed twice a day. The penis especially must be washed very carefully. The foreskin should be gently pulled back, as the seminal fluid can form a yellow-white coat underneath, which smells unpleasant. With lukewarm water, it can be washed off easily.

Exercise caution with soap in this spot, as it can irritate sensitive skin. Just use water or, if anything, a mild, unscented cleanser.

Especially for Girls

Girls and women should avoid using soap to clean their genital area, as the sensitive skin of the labia can be prone to itching and burning. And certainly no soap should go into the vagina. For a thorough cleaning, even when menstruating, you only need warm water and at most a mild, unscented cleanser.

Good hygiene is very important during your period. A woman has several options: She can use special pads (sanitary napkins), which are like small diapers that adhere to the underwear. Although these pads come in different sizes, they can be inconvenient, for example, when exercising or playing sports.

An alternative to pads is tampons. These are pushed into the vagina and typically you won't feel them at all while they're in. Tampons absorb the menstrual fluid while inside the body and then can be pulled out again by a small string. Any woman can use tampons, and they come in different sizes. Even very young girls don't have to go without them, as there are tampons available that are small enough to fit through the narrow opening in the hymen.

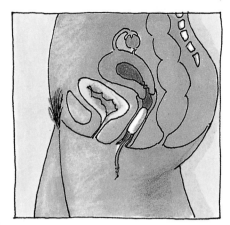

The tampon absorbs menstrual fluid inside the vagina.

Other options growing in popularity among today's women include menstrual cups and period-proof underwear. Feel free to do research on your own if these are options you'd like to consider!

Tampons and pads must be changed several times a day—depending on how heavy the bleeding is. If you do not change the tampon often enough, you can get sick. So please never skimp on tampons.

It's best if you buy your first pads, tampons, cups, or period panties with a grown woman. She can give you a few tips, "woman to woman."

I've got to try these all out!

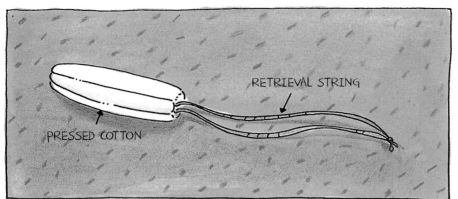

The **tampon** is a cone of stuffed cotton. It is pushed into the vagina where it absorbs the menstrual fluid. The string hanging from it can be used to pull it back out. Tampons come in different sizes and some include special applicators.

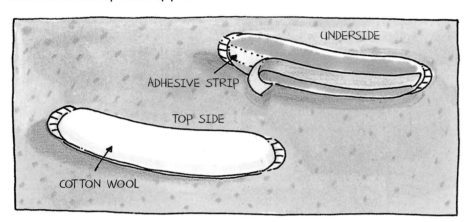

The **panty liner** consists of cotton wool. It is small and thin and attaches with an adhesive strip to the panties. It is well suited to adding an extra layer of protection while wearing a tampon. In the last days of the period, which tend to be lighter, it is often enough on its own.

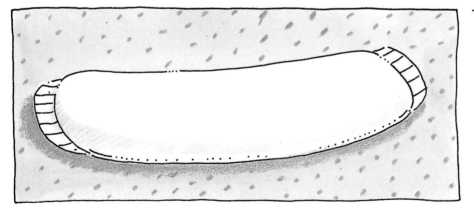

The **pad (sanitary napkin)** consists, like the panty liner, of cotton wool and plastic underwear protection, but is larger and thicker. It alone is sufficient as bleeding protection on all days of the period. Pads are available in a wide variety of designs and sizes.

Love—and What It Entails

Love—What Exactly is It?

When asked to define love, adults will often struggle to answer. Love is the many incredibly beautiful and sometimes terrible feelings that one person can feel for another.

Love is not always necessarily between a man and a woman, although that is the case for most, and this is called **heterosexual** love. Two men or two women can also be in love. This is called **homosexual** love. Men who love men are called **gay**. Women who love women are called **lesbians**. Men and women who love both men and women are **bisexual**. People may also identify as **queer** (not exclusively heterosexual), **pansexual** (attraction to people in general, not specifically because of gender), **asexual** (not necessarily attracted to anyone sexually), **aromantic** (not attracted to anyone romantically), and a number of other identities/terms.

Some people are afraid and intolerant of homosexuality and other sexual orientations. There is no reason for that—it is perfectly natural. Ultimately, everyone should be allowed

to love whoever they love regardless of gender.

When you're in love, others will often notice before you do! All of a sudden, you're talking only about one particular person. You're trying to get closer to them, and you look at them as often as possible. And everything else in your life might suddenly seem unimportant. Even the most amazing games and the most exciting TV shows don't interest you anymore. But if you're really in love, you also feel a bunch of other things: Your heart beats wildly when you think about this person; when you see them, you might feel shaky with excitement and hardly able to speak; you might dream about this person almost every night!

Love is...

...like butterflies in your head.

...like airplanes in your stomach.

...like floating on pink clouds.

...like a walk through the land of plenty.

...like a burning ice cube.

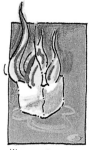

...like sunshine at night.

...like a sickness for which there's no medicine.

We say people in love...

...are smitten.

...only have eyes (and ears) for their beloved.

...are in their own world.

...see everything through rose-colored glasses.

...hear wedding bells chiming.

...have their heads in the clouds.

...can't think straight.

How Do I Just Say It?

At first it can be very difficult to talk about your feelings for someone with that person. It can take a lot of courage to tell someone: "I've fallen in love with you."

If saying it with words sounds too scary, you can also show your love through your actions.

You can make an effort to please the other person, tell them through glances how much you like them, be a good listener, or share in meaningful activities together.

But it can also sometimes happen that the person you love doesn't notice how much in love you are. A few small tricks can help you to let them know: You could ask your best friend to relay the message; or you could write them a short love letter.

Despite your best efforts, the person you love might not react the way you hope. Sometimes it's because they don't feel the same way. Other times, they may already be in love with someone else.

If you love someone but they don't love you back, that can be very painful. Unfortunately, there's nothing you can do about this. Everyone feels lovesick at one time or another in life. When that happens, it can be good to talk to someone about it—to a friend, or maybe even with an older sibling or a parent.

The pain and sadness of unrequited love are as much a part of the experience of love as joy and racing hearts. Love is a strange mix of happiness and fear because everyone's always a little afraid of losing the other person.

Love Requires Patience and Lots of Time

Part of love is always a wish: that two people can be together as often as possible. But that's not enough for those in love. They want to be close to each other. That is very important. People in love are full of curiosity about one another; they want to know everything about the other person; they wants to see, hear, smell, and touch the one they love.

The first time your hand touches that of another, or when you gently run your fingers through their hair, the things you feel are usually hard to describe. Some people say there's an electricity with that first touch, or that it's like a firecracker going off on New Year's Eve.

A strange tingling goes through the entire body, from the roots of your hair to the tips of your toes. Or it's like hot and cold water running over your back at the same time. Your knees begin to shake and you think you're going to fall over.

The closer you get, the more you touch, the crazier this feeling becomes.

And when kissing on the lips, some forget to breathe for a few moments.

In order for lovers to concentrate on these feelings completely, they need a lot of peace and time. There's no need to rush love. And that is why it is very important to go step by step. The slower it goes, the better you get to know each other. If one person is in too big a hurry, then chances are it's not really love. Love means caring about what the other person wants, not just what you want.

Sometimes even adults seem to forget. It happens often that adults, especially men, force children or young people into acts of love. They want to do everything that a couple does: cuddle, kiss, and have sex with each other.

But this has nothing to do with love; and actually, it's a crime. If you don't want to do those things with someone, it is your right to say no, whether it is a stranger, a relative, a friend, or an acquaintance.

Girls and women are most at risk. Some men use violence or manipulation in order to have sex with others. This is called rape. It is important to note that boys can be sexually abused, too.

If you have been sexually harassed or assaulted, you shouldn't keep this to yourself—though you may feel scared or ashamed. No matter what, know that this abuse was not your fault. If possible, and if you feel safe doing so, talk to your best friend, to a trusted relative, or your favorite teacher about it. They can help you decide if you should speak to the police. This also applies if the person who hurt you is a family member or a friend. A person who sexually abuses another is sick and requires professional help.

Cuddling and Kissing are Wonderful

Most boys and girls fall in love many times before they grow up. When you get a bit older and have experienced romance for many weeks or months, there's a point at which kissing and holding hands don't feel like enough. Cuddling and caressing one another feels so nice that it's natural to want to take things further.

Lovers feel the desire to undress and to caress each other's whole body, even their genitals. This deepens the feelings of pleasure that a couple can experience together. When a couple is sexually aroused in this way, they each will experience distinct changes to their body. In men, the penis becomes larger and harder; he gets an erection. Sometimes the glans will even secrete a small amount of fluid. This is called **pre-ejaculate**.

Women's bodies also change. The clitoris and labia become larger and the vagina becomes wet. This is how lovers' bodies prepare themselves for **sexual intercourse**, or **sex** (or to "sleep together").

However, when boys and girls touch one another for the very first time, they often don't jump straight to intercourse. At that stage, it can be enough to simply caress each other all over and to enjoy the nice feelings in doing so. This is called **petting**.

What Happens During Sexual Intercourse

At the Climax . . .

When a man and woman desire one another and decide to sleep together, the man will push his penis into the woman's vagina.

In doing so, the foreskin is pulled back. The sensitive glans at the end of the penis becomes even more aroused by this. At the same time, the woman's labia, the entrance to the vagina, and the clitoris and its surrounding area become stimulated by the man's penis and his movements.

The pleasure men and women feel during intercourse is hard to describe. And because both of them want to have more of this feeling, the man again and again pulls his penis out and pushes it back in. The man and woman hardly know how they should express their joy. They begin to moan, laugh, scream, or giggle in quite a goofy way.

It also can be that they begin to cry with happiness.

Finally, the man and woman reach the climax of their feelings. They each experience an orgasm, though not always at the same time. For a woman, this often requires intense stimulation of the clitoris. Most women cannot reach orgasm from vaginal intercourse alone. For a man, an orgasm is expressed through ejaculation. His penis secretes sperm, which are suspended in seminal fluid that was produced in the testes. Many millions—sometimes even hundreds of millions—of sperm are transported from the penis into the woman's vagina.

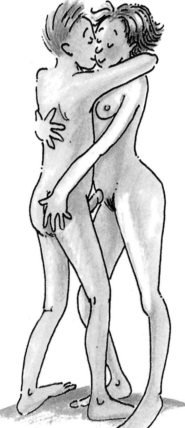

The First Time

You should not expect too much from your first time having sexual intercourse. The first time can be difficult or awkward—and not as beautiful as both imagined it would be. Often this is because the couple is too inexperienced or has too little time and cannot act undisturbed.

However, all the fuss around sex also has an impact. In men, the pressure to perform can make it so he can't insert his penis because it won't stay erect. But this is quite normal and can happen to anyone. In women, that same pressure can make pleasure during sex somewhat elusive.

Quite often it happens that people are afraid of doing something wrong the first time. Suddenly, both lovers are as stressed as if struggling with a difficult school assignment. They find they cannot concentrate on the tenderness and pleasure of the moment and become insecure or overwhelmed.

To prevent these roadblocks, men and women should very slowly familiarize themselves with the other's body. Talk to each other and say what feels good and what doesn't, what you're afraid of and what makes you uncomfortable. Only then can you come to tenderness and trust needed for romantic, mutually pleasurable sex.

At no point should a couple in love feel forced or obligated to sleep together. Physical affection comprised of caressing and kissing can be beautiful and more than enough. When you're both feeling pressured to have sex, more often than not your bodies will tense up.

Because of this, the first time can be painful for women and girls. The hymen, which in young girls seals off the vagina except for a small hole, will often tear; some bleeding the first time is common. This in itself is not bad.

But if it really hurts, it is better to stop and postpone the first attempt to a different day. Healthy and enjoyable sex takes practice and communication; it's best when you help and listen to one another. That's why it's important always to talk about everything, even if it's difficult.

The Fastest Sperm Wins

When the man ejaculates during intercourse, the semen enters the woman's vagina. From there the sperm swim through the uterus and into the fallopian tube. The sperm are always in search of an egg that can be fertilized. Once they find one, the fastest sperm penetrates the egg cell and merges with it. This is called fertilization. As soon as the egg has been fertilized, the embryonic membrane becomes impenetrable to all other sperm.

This fertilization almost always takes place in the upper part of the fallopian tube. This is because a woman's eggs are capable of being fertilized for roughly twenty-four hours after ovulation. On the other hand, the sperm can remain viable in the woman's body for up to seven days. This means the egg cell can be fertilized days after intercourse.

The fertilized egg moves through the fallopian tube into the uterus and embeds itself in the mucous membrane there. From the tiny embryo a baby begins to grow: The woman is pregnant.

What the Spermatozoon Looks Like

The fluid that is ejected from the penis during ejaculation looks mostly milky white. It can be thin or viscous and sticky. But it is only the smallest part of a man's spermatozoon. The largest part is the lubricant and nutrient fluid, which sustains the semen and ensures that it can swim in the woman's body.

If you know that a single ejaculation can release many millions of individual sperm from the man's body, you can imagine how small a single spermatozoon is. Only under a microscope can you see that each spermatozoon looks similar to a tadpole. The sperm has a head in which the cell nucleus is found. This is key for fertilization of the female egg because it stores the father's genetic information and will determine half of the genetic makeup of the child. The tail of the sperm can move quite quickly like a fish's and ensures that the semen can swim through the woman's uterus and into the fallopian tubes.

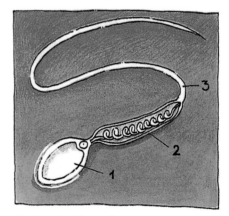

1   Head with nucleus
2   Middle part
3   Tail

Two Pairs of Twins

You've probably seen twins before. One in eighty pregnant women will give birth to two babies at the same time instead of just one. Maybe there are twins at your school or in your group of friends. If you've met multiple pairs of twins, you might notice that some pairs look almost exactly alike, and others not at all. Some pairs of twins are the same gender and others are one boy and one girl.

This is because there are two different types of twins: identical and fraternal.

Sometimes an egg cell divides immediately after being fertilized by a man's sperm. Despite this division, the egg is not broken. Quite the opposite: the egg has become two fully viable, fertilized ova, each identical to the other. Both will nest in the uterus and develop simultaneously into two babies. Because the ova are identical, the babies will have the same gender and look very much alike. This is how identical twins are made.

Fraternal twins occur when two sperm fertilize two viable ova, one in each of a woman's fallopian tubes. The result is two babies at the same time. They can be of the same gender, or one boy and one girl, and they will resemble each other only as much as siblings typically do, since they have developed from two completely different sperm and egg cells.

Weiner	Penis
Balls	Testes
Boner	Erection
Cum	Ejaculation
Spunk	Ejaculate
Ball Sack	Scrotum
Crotch	Mons Pubis
Oven	Uterus
Box	Vagina
Kitty	Vulva
Bean	Clitoris
Period	Menstruation
Doing it	Coitus
Rubber	Condom

Sex, Pregnancy, and Contraception

Truths and Half-Truths about Pregnancy

You've already learned how a woman becomes pregnant: A man's spermatozoon goes into the woman's egg cell and fertilizes it.

When the man's penis is inserted into the woman's vagina, the sperm have it very easy when it comes to reaching the egg. The risk of unintentionally conceiving a child when having sex is very high—much higher than most boys and girls believe.

Therefore it often happens that unwanted babies are conceived during sexual intercourse. This can happen when girls are very young—as young as nine, if the girl has begun or is about to begin her first menstrual cycle. Of course, the circumstances that lead to pregnancy at that age are extreme. But even pregnancy at sixteen can invite a world of problems. Consider: If the parents of babies that are themselves still children or adolescents, it is very unlikely that they will be able to care for a child on their own. They have to attend school, they don't have a home of their own, and they probably aren't earning money yet.

Therefore, it's best to ensure that girls don't get pregnant before reaching adulthood. To do this, it's important to learn about all the available preventative options, or forms of **contraception**.

But for many it is not entirely clear when or how to use a contraceptive. Some believe that young girls cannot get pregnant. But that isn't true. And it isn't the only misconception around pregnancy.

REALLY?

SEXUAL EDUCATION

F. Only grown women can get pregnant

Girls as young as nine can get pregnant. √

F. Girls can only first get pregnant after their first period.

It can also happen beforehand, as long as there is an egg cell that can be fertilized. √

F. Nothing can happen the first time.

The risk is as great as at any later time. √

F. Girls can only get pregnant if they have an orgasm during sex.

The female orgasm has nothing to with fertilization of the egg cell. √

F. Nothing can happen if it you only get a hand job.

After a boy ejaculates, sperm can be transferred to the woman's vagina by a hand and still fertilize an egg. √

F. Taking a birth control pill after sex protects against pregnancy.

Birth control pills only work if you take them regularly as prescribed by a doctor. √

F. Adolescents don't need to use any protection.

Adolescents must protect themselves from unwanted pregnancy. √

The Pull-Out Method

There are young people and also adults that don't use contraceptives, but don't want children. They trust that the man can prevent pregnancy by withdrawing his penis from the vagina right before ejaculation. However, this is a very unreliable method. That's because even before ejaculation a small amount of semen can spill out of the opening in the glans without the man noticing.

This "trick" is known as **coitus interruptus**, and more commonly referred to as the **pull-out method**. It's not a particularly romantic gesture, given that the man is withdrawing right at the pinnacle of intercourse, when feelings are otherwise the strongest and most tender.

If someone always has to make sure to pull out in time, then the couple cannot really concentrate on the pleasure of sex.

 This method of contraception is absolutely unreliable and not at all recommended.

The Condom

A **condom** looks similar to an uninflated balloon. It consists of wafer-thin rubber and is pulled over the man's erect penis. This rubber shield ensures that the semen does not enter the woman's vagina. That way fertilization cannot occur.

Condoms are considered very reliable contraceptives when used properly. When opening the condom wrapper, you must take care not to damage the rubber with your fingernail.

It's not always easy at first to slip the condom on. Each boy should therefore, before he sleeps with a girl for the first time, take a condom, look at it, and practice slipping it on by himself. Those who have a little bit of practice will soon be able to handle them quite well.

First you need to pull back the foreskin from over the glans. Then take the still rolled-up condom and slip it on, carefully unrolling it over the erect penis. You must not pull the condom on too tight, as there must still be room at the tip for catching the seminal fluid. Good condoms have a sizeable reservoir at the tip. This is a small space that looks like a point. After ejaculation the semen is collected there.

The most common error in the use of condoms happens when they are placed upside down on the glans and cannot be unrolled. Make sure you are unrolling the whole condom!

1 Carefully tear open the package and remove the condom. Make sure it doesn't tear!
2 Press the reservoir together, push back the foreskin, and place the condom over the glans.
3 Unroll the condom toward the base of the penis, as far down as possible, and hold it tightly when inserting the penis into the vagina.

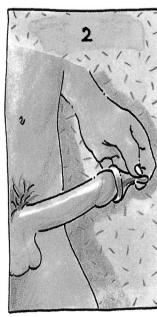

Each condom should only be used once. After intercourse, when the penis is pulled out of the vagina, the condom should still be in place. As you withdraw, it's best if you hold the bottom of the condom tightly, so that it does not slip off of the penis. Even after ejaculation, the penis should not be reinserted into the vagina without a new condom. This is because semen can remain in the urethra for many hours and could still fertilize the egg cell.

You can buy condoms in supermarkets, drug stores, pharmacies, or department stores. They are even available in vending machines. Good condoms always have an expiration date on the box. Condoms that are coated with a **lubricant** are the easiest to apply and can also make sex more comfortable for the woman.

 At first, a bit of practice is necessary. But then the condom is a very good method of contraception.

Where's my condom?

Chemical Contraceptives

In pharmacies and drugstores, there are **chemical contraceptives**, or **spermicides**, that you can buy without a prescription. They are available in various forms: as suppositories, gels, foams, creams, or sponges. Chemical contraceptives are inserted into the vagina before sexual intercourse. They prevent the sperm from reaching the egg cells.

Chemical contraceptives are easier to use than condoms. You don't need a tutorial or to practice. But they also have disadvantages.

They are not considered to be entirely reliable contraceptives. Plus, after application, the spermicide can sometimes cause both partners to experience itching and burning on their genitals.

> *Pregnancy prevention with chemical contraceptives is convenient, but not particularly reliable. It's best to combine with other means of prevention, such as a diaphragm. However, the ingredients in some spermicides can actually damage condoms, so only combine condoms with chemical contraceptives as indicated on the package!*

Birth Control Pills

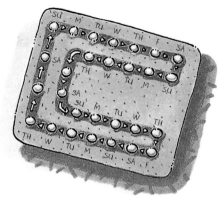

Birth control pills are tablets containing hormones that prevent ovulation from taking place. In addition, they thicken the mucus in the cervix so that no semen can reach the uterus. If, however, an egg is somehow fertilized, the "pill" blocks the hormones that would otherwise allow the egg to implant in the uterine lining. The pill is a very good protection against an unwanted pregnancy, but only if the instructions are followed exactly.

Typically, a girl or woman will take one pill a day, every day for three weeks. Depending on the kind of birth control, the fourth week consists of either **placebo** pills (pills with no medical effect) or no pills at all. This allows menstruation to take place that week.

Birth control pills are prescribed by a **gynecologist** after a consultation and examination. If the patient is healthy, she receives a prescription for the tablets. Her parents do not have to be asked for permission.

WOOOSH!

Any woman who takes the pill must undergo regular examinations. It can take the body time to adjust to the medication, which can sometimes. cause headaches, nausea, or tightness in the chest. If these symptoms don't go away, the gynecologist can prescribe a different birth control pill.

 The pill is the safest contraceptive, even for young girls—if taking the medicine as prescribed. The downside is that the hormones can have many side effects, especially in women who smoke.

while hormonal IUDs slowly release the same kind of hormones found in the pill. An IUD can remain in the uterus for up to ten years, at which point the doctor must replace it with a new one.

For young girls, the IUD is not always the best contraceptive—especially the copper version, which can cause pain and heavier bleeding during your period.

The IUD is a contraceptive that remains in the body for a longer period of time. This method is not recommended for young women.

The IUD

An **intrauterine device**, or **IUD**, is made of plastic. Some are wrapped in a thin copper wire, while others emit hormones. They are available in many different shapes and sizes. Earlier versions looked like spirals, but the ones most commonly used today are shaped like small ship anchors. An IUD is inserted into the uterus by a doctor. Copper IUDs cause an inflammatory reaction that prevents a fertilized egg from implanting in the uterine lining,

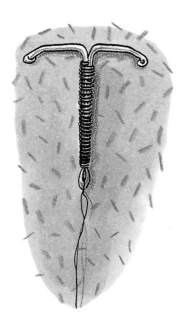

The Diaphragm

The **diaphragm**, also called the cervical cap, consists of a soft rubber cap with a flexible wire edge. Before sex, the diaphragm is rubbed with a spermicidal cream or gel and inserted into the vagina. It sits like an elastic wall in front of the cervix. This physically prevents the semen from entering the uterus, thus preventing fertilization. The spermicide provides additional security.

After sex, the diaphragm must remain in the vagina for at least eight hours. Then it should be removed, washed, and treated with a special solution to keep it elastic. The diaphragm must be fitted by a doctor, since there are different sizes.

 The diaphragm is a very good type of protection if applied properly. It is not, however, very easy to use.

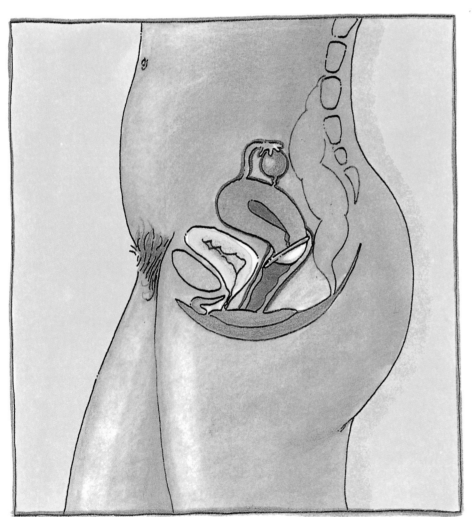

The diaphragm closes off the cervix, preventing semen from entering the uterus.

The Natural Method

Every twenty-eight days an egg travels from a woman's ovary into the fallopian tube. Only immediately afterwards, for about twenty-four hours, is the egg ready for fertilization. This means there are days on which a woman cannot become pregnant because there is no viable egg waiting in the fallopian tube.

In order to use **the natural method**, also called the rhythm method, a woman must carefully track her monthly cycle. To be certain about when ovulation takes place, she must use a thermometer to take her temperature inside her vagina each morning. It can be helpful to record these values on a graph. If her temperature suddenly rises by 0.7 to 1.1 degrees Fahrenheit, that means she is ovulating. This means she must take extra precautions if she plans to have sex around that time but doesn't wish to become pregnant.

In addition, a woman can monitor the natural discharge from her vagina. Normally, it is thick and white. During ovulation, however, it is thinner and almost clear.

Additionally, if you take it between the tips of your fingers and then spread your fingers apart, the discharge should form a thread. During this time, you and your partner should not sleep together without contraceptives. When the discharge thickens and becomes white again, your "infertile days" have begun.

A gynecologist can provide you with graphs for recording your daily temperature and discharge quality.

For young girls, the natural method of contraception is not recommended as their cycles are too irregular. It also takes a lot of discipline and organization to remember to take your temperature and monitor your body every day.

Using the natural method to prevent pregnancy places limits on when you can safely have sex. If you are confident you are in an infertile period, you do not need any contraception at that time. Nevertheless, this method is reliable only if the woman closely monitors herself and if her cycle is regular. This method is not suitable for young girls.

Emergency Solutions: The "Morning-After Pill"

Despite your best efforts to prevent pregnancy, things can sometimes still go wrong: The condom breaks; you forget to take the pill; or for whatever reason you find yourself having had unsafe sex. When this happens, the woman should go to the pharmacy immediately to request the "**morning-after pill**." This pill should be taken within seventy-two hours after intercourse, and preferably within the first twelve to twenty-four hours. The morning-after pill can prevent or delay ovulation but cannot prevent an already fertilized egg from implanting in the uterine lining.

The Rule Holds

If you miss a period, that isn't necessarily a sign that you're pregnant. Sometimes stress, age, or other factors can cause the menstrual cycle to be irregular. However, it's always good to be sure if you think there's a possibility you could be pregnant. You can buy a pregnancy test at any pharmacy and administer it at home. If the test is positive, or if it is negative but you want to be extra certain, you should see a doctor to discuss your health and your options.

Abortion

An **abortion** is performed when a woman decides to terminate her pregnancy. Depending on where she lives, and the laws in place there, she should consult with a trusted doctor or visit a respected reproductive health center like Planned Parenthood, which can answer questions about the procedure and its cost.

The abortion itself is only a minor operation, usually done as an outpatient procedure. The earlier it is performed, the lower the risk. During the procedure, the cervix is dilated and any tissue implanted in the uterus is sucked out. Even though the pain is not too intense in most cases, an abortion can still be a difficult experience. In many places there is a social stigma against choosing to terminate a pregnancy, which can lead to feelings of guilt and shame for the woman.

About a week after the operation, the doctor conducts a follow-up examination. An abortion does not affect a woman's ability to later become pregnant and bear healthy children.

Fertility Issues

Many couples struggle to conceive children. There many causes: Sometimes the man's sperm or the woman's egg are simply unsuitable for fertilization; the man's sperm count might be too low; the woman may be unable to ovulate; or her anatomy may be particularly resistant to conception.

These in turn may relate to hormone deficiencies. Previously, we described hormones as tiny messages sent from the brain through the bloodstream to tell the reproductive system what to do. Our sex organs also "write" their own messages, sending them through the bloodstream to other places in the body.

Smoking too much, drinking too much alcohol, getting too little sleep, working too much, a poor diet, a long illness, or certain medications can all disrupt hormonal health. There are also genetic conditions, present at birth, that can affect someone's endocrine (or hormonal) system.

If something is not working properly with these hormonal signals in the body, fertility can be impacted. As a result, men's bodies may not produce enough sperm, or women's egg cells may not be viable.

Sometimes a doctor can help by prescribing the man or woman hormonal supplements in pill form. Often these can restore function to the sexual organs.

If, despite the hormonal treatments, a couple is still unable to conceive, a doctor may suggest a method called **in-vitro fertilization**. First, the doctor performs a minor operation in which s/he removes an egg cell from one of the woman's ovaries. This cell is then fertilized by the man's sperm, outside of the body. Then the egg is implanted into the woman's uterus. Sometimes this works right away, and other times it takes several tries.

Even Healthy People Should Go to the Doctor

A Doctor for All Cases

You've probably been to the doctor before. Maybe because of a cold, or a stomach ache, or because you were injured.

The doctor you see the most is usually your family doctor because they're who you almost always go to first, and they can help with many kinds of illnesses.

However, there are also doctors that only treat certain issues. As boys and girls start to grow up, seeing these specialists becomes more and more common.

Girls, once they begin puberty, should regularly visit the **gynecologist**, a doctor who specializes in women's reproductive health.

Gynecologists are the experts when it comes to treating anything related to the reproductive system. They can advise women on contraception, adjust diaphragms and insert IUDs, and prescribe birth control pills. Pregnant women in particular will visit doctors who specialize in both gynecology and **obstetrics** (the medical science of childbirth). These specialists are called OB/GYNs for short, and will help make sure the baby is developing normally throughout the pregnancy. They will also be present for the birth, if the mother chooses to give birth in a hospital.

For boys, it's somewhat different. There is not a particular doctor who specializes in male reproductive health. However, some doctors do specialize in urology, which is the study of the urinary system (which includes the penis). These doctors are called **urologists**. However, they also treat urinary issues in women.

The Examination

Regular visits to the gynecologist are very important. It's normal to feel nervous before you go, especially if it's your first time. If you're afraid to go alone, you can always take along your best friend, a sister, or even your mother. For the doctor, examining your genitals and answering any questions you have is totally routine, so there's nothing to worry about.

This way, if something changes or something strange happens to you later on, you'll know an expert you can talk to.

Wasn't bad at all. I could go again.

The same applies for boys. Sometimes the testicles do not develop correctly, or the foreskin cannot be pulled all the way back from the glans. This is not an illness, rather a small growth defect. The urologist or dermatologist can help by making a small incision—otherwise you won't be able to wash your penis correctly. Additionally, a tight foreskin can hurt or break during intercourse.

Many **sexually transmitted diseases/ infections** (STDs or STIs) begin with an itching or burning sensation. It is also common to experience unusual discharge from the vagina, for girls, or from the urethra, for boys. At that point it is high time to see the gynecologist or urologist, because these conditions are unlikely to go away on their own. Without medical attention they can worsen or even cause lasting damage.

The doctor will take a swab from the vagina or the urethra and examine it under a microscope.

When it comes to your reproductive health, it is not advisable to rely on your friends for answers. Everything concerning the **genitals** is a case for the doctor. They are experts.

When the gynecologist or urologist examines you, s/he sees your genitalia and palpates them. Often s/he takes a swab. In doing so, the doctor takes some fluid from the vagina or the urethra with a small stick. It will be examined for pathogens. If the doctor finds something, s/he can prescribe the right medicine.

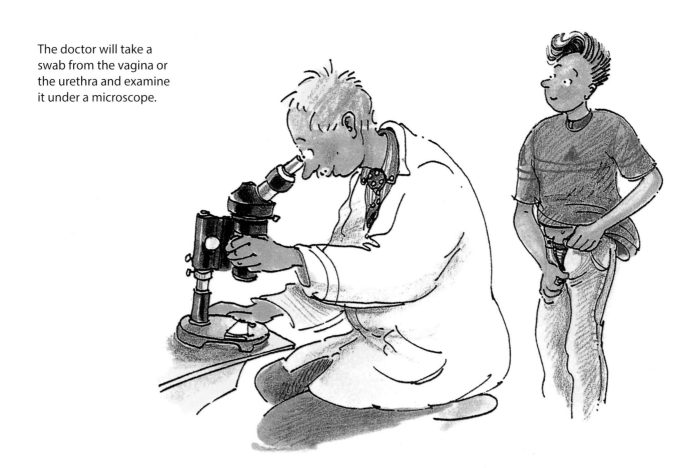

The doctor will take a swab from the vagina or the urethra and examine it under a microscope.

HIV and AIDS

Many sexually transmitted infections are quickly noticeable. When your symptoms are itching and burning on your genitals, you can tell right away that something is wrong. You can go to the doctor and get treatment.

But there is one infection that is not technically an STI, although it is transmitted primarily during sexual intercourse. It is a virus called **HIV** (human immunodeficiency virus). If left untreated it can lead to a very serious, fatal condition called **AIDS**.

AIDS is an abbreviation for acquired immunodeficiency syndrome.

AIDS has devastating effects on the immune system. It infects—then depletes—your body's T-cells, which are typically responsible for fending off diseases.

In healthy people, these immune cells will work to fight off a cold, for example, without outside help; they are like your body's homemade medication. When these cells are no longer functional, a simple runny nose can escalate to a deadly case of pneumonia.

Medicine has made great leaps in recent years: There are now medications available that will not only control the symptoms of HIV—preventing opportunistic infections—but they will also reduce the presence of the virus so much that it is undetectable in the blood, and prevent the spread of HIV to others. Incredibly, these drugs can keep HIV from becoming AIDS. In fact, since the advent of these treatments, the progression of HIV to AIDS has become increasingly rare.

Nevertheless, a total cure has not yet been discovered, and thus there are still fatal cases of AIDS each year, especially among those whose HIV has gone undiagnosed or untreated.

What's tricky is the fact that HIV can lie dormant for years, hidden in the body. Before the outbreak of the infection, there are usually no symptoms. This means an HIV-infected person can potentially infect others without knowing it. That is why it is very important if you are sexually active to be tested regularly for HIV and other STIs/STDs.

HIV can only be transmitted when an infected person's blood, semen, or vaginal fluid enters into the body of a healthy individual. This can happen during sexual intercourse, through a blood transfusion (rarer now that doctors know to test blood donations first), through reusing needles, or when an HIV-positive mother passes the virus to her unborn child.

To protect yourself during sexual intercourse, you should use condoms every time!

Always remember that an HIV infection may not have any symptoms at first. That's why you and your sexual partners should be sure to get tested regularly.

If you know someone who has HIV or AIDS, there is no reason to avoid them. As mentioned, HIV can only be transmitted through blood, semen, or vaginal fluid—and not, for example, through hugging or shaking hands. People who are HIV-positive should be treated with as much compassion and respect as any healthy person.

Pregnancy—
from a Cell to a Whole Person

The First Moment Decides

Now we're going to look at exactly what happens once an egg has been fertilized. Obviously, it will develop into a baby. But it's a long journey to birth.

It all starts in the fallopian tube. The sperm must swim through it until it comes across an egg it can fertilize. Only one of the many sperm cells that enter the vagina through ejaculation will reach the egg. And when the two meet, they join together immediately. A barrier forms around them at lightning speed. No other sperm cell can penetrate it.

When the sperm and egg are fused together, the genetic material contained in them merges. **Genetic material** refers to everything that a child receives from their parents: hair color, skin color, whether they will be short or tall, and many other things. In addition, the sperm determines whether the baby will be a boy or a girl.

If the tiny sperm were as large as a pinhead, then the egg would be the size of a beach ball.

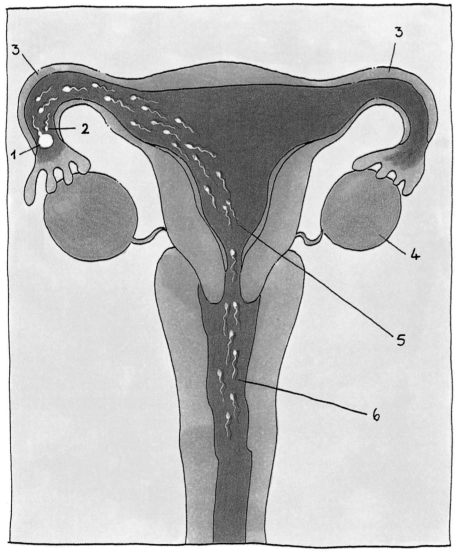

1 Egg being fertilized
2 Sperm
3 Fallopian tube
4 Ovary
5 Uterus
6 Vagina

What People and Snowmen Have in Common

Together the egg and the sperm form the very first cell of the baby's body. Cells are the smallest building blocks of every living organism. They are so tiny that they are impossible to see with the naked eye, and there are an infinite number of them. Imagine a cell within the body as a snowflake. When you build a snowman, you can no longer count the snowflakes it contains.

After the first cell is made from the sperm and egg, it divides. There are now two new cells. Everything about them is identical to the first cell. They hold together tightly, as if with tiny arms, and keep on dividing. Two become four, then eight, then sixteen. Their number multiplies rapidly.

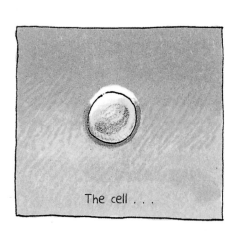

The cell . . .

. . . divides itself . . .

After just a few days, there are so many that you no longer can count them. This collection of cells is called the embryo. The embryo moves slowly from the fallopian tube into the uterus, where it adheres to the uterine lining.

The embryo forms a layer around itself called the amniotic sac. This is filled with amniotic fluid. The baby will be suspended in this fluid up until birth. The amniotic sac protects the baby from hard impacts, like when the mother falls, for example.

Feeding through the Umbilical Cord

Being surrounded completely by amniotic fluid is not a problem for the embryo—it doesn't need to breathe. Oxygen and everything else the embryo needs to grow is stored in the **placenta**, an organ that develops in the womb in order to supply the baby with nutrients from the mother's blood throughout pregnancy.

Those nutrients are passed to the embryo through the **umbilical cord**. This is a kind of hose that runs from the placenta all the way to the embryo's stomach. Every person, even as an adult, can still see the place their umbilical cord was once attached: their **belly button**!

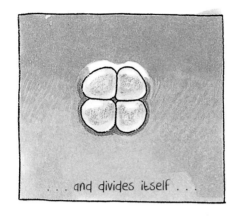

... and divides itself ...

... and divides itself ...

The Mother's Body Prepares Itself

Once the embryo has found its place in the uterus, the placenta produces a special hormone called **human chorionic gonadotropin** (hCG). This hormone sends a message to the woman's body, telling it that a baby has begun to grow.

And now the woman's entire body prepares itself for pregnancy. In order for the uterus to be a hospitable home for the baby, it is very important that the mother's monthly menstrual bleeding cease. This is why a missed period is often a sign that pregnancy has begun.

The rush of hormones that comes with the presence of a baby can have some interesting effects on the mother. In the first stage of pregnancy, it often happens that the woman has a strange taste in her mouth. She might feel sick to her stomach. She might develop cravings for certain foods, or weird combinations of food, for example, salty fish with chocolate.

... and divides itself ...

Why don't you like this? I thought you were pregnant!

The woman's breasts also begin to grow and might also feel more tender than usual. This is because the milk ducts are preparing to produce milk for after the baby's birth.

Because this whole adjustment places a great burden on the body, mothers are often very tired and weary. They might grumble about things that would otherwise not bother them. They might feel especially emotional. This is perfectly normal.

It is important for an expectant mother to take extra care with her own health. She should not smoke or drink alcohol, as these indulgences will enter into the embryo's bloodstream as well. This can be very dangerous because they can harm the baby's growth.

Even more dangerous are certain drugs or medications. Some pills contain substances that can kill an embryo or make it sick. Therefore, pregnant women should only take drugs prescribed by their doctor.

Especially in the first few weeks after the start of the pregnancy, the woman should be very careful. She shouldn't strain herself at work or through intense physical activity, for example, otherwise she could lose her baby. When a baby dies before the twentieth week of pregnancy, it's called a **miscarriage**.

The Baby Grows in the Womb

In the first weeks, the teeny-tiny child, or **fetus**, looks nothing like a person. They are simply a cluster of cells in the womb.

In the first month, cells that will become the brain, retina, lungs, and liver begin to form. Despite the fact that the fetus is still so tiny, it begins to grow limbs. The head starts to form. Tiny stubs show where the arms and legs will grow.

One month after fertilization, the fetus is about one-fifth of an inch long.

The fetus is now as big as a pea …

In the second month, the first signs of the ears appear on the fetus's head. Even the palate and the tooth ridges are forming. Later the teeth will grow there. On the legs, the still small stubs begin to gradually grow into feet. The tiny arm stubs show the beginnings of hands.

Two months after fertilization, the fetus is still tiny. Usually, it is between one and one and a half inches and weighs less than two grams. That's as much as a sheet of paper.

… and now the size of a piece of candy.

In the third month, the woman's uterus begins to stretch because now the baby needs more space. It is now three and a half inches long and weighs about half an ounce. As the uterus grows, the woman's stomach also becomes larger. The fetus now clearly shows the first signs of fingers and toes. A nose has grown on the face. You can also see the mouth and eye sockets. Now the fetus really looks like a tiny person.

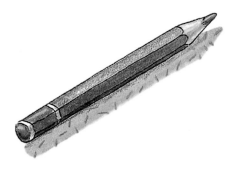

In the third month, the fetus is about as long as a colored pencil you've been using for a while . . .

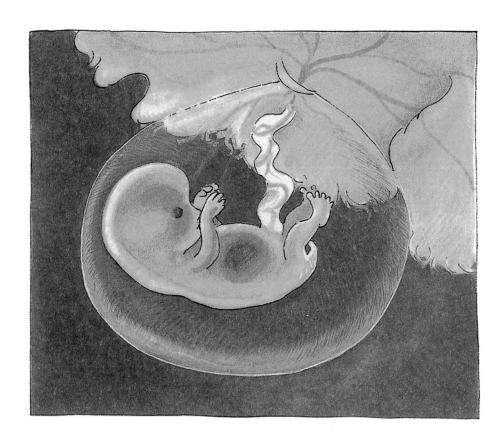

In the fourth month, the baby is about six inches long. When the doctor now places a stethoscope on the mother's stomach, s/he can hear the fetus's heartbeat. The heart beats approximately 160 times per minute, twice as fast as an adult human's. The baby's whole body now grows soft hair, even on its face. But in most cases, this falls out before birth.

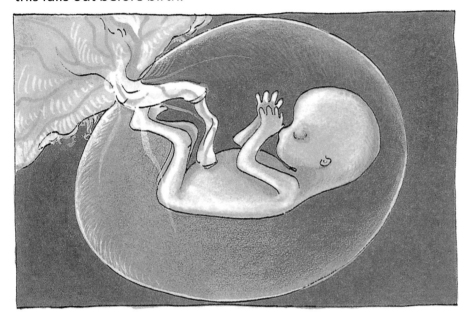

. . . and in the fourth month, it is the length of a brand new colored pencil!

In the fifth month, the mother sometimes feels the baby kicking in her stomach. The womb will have a narrower shape, as the baby is now almost ten inches long and weighs over ten and half ounces.

By now, the baby is as big as an eggplant.

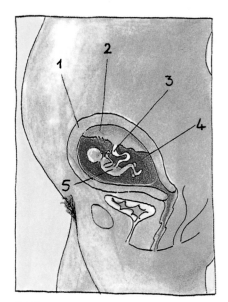

1 Uterus
2 Placenta
3 Umbilical cord
4 Amniotic sac with amniotic fluid
5 Embryo/fetus

In the sixth month after fertilization, the baby is growing rapidly, but is still pretty light. It weighs just 21.2 ounces. Sometimes the mother can feel the feet or other body parts through the wall of her abdomen. When she places a hand on her stomach, the baby can sense her touch and will often react. In addition, the baby can now hear and recognize its parents' voices.

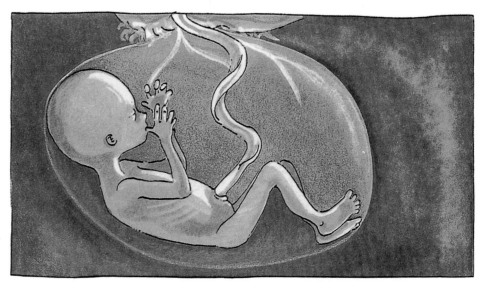

In the seventh month, the baby is almost sixteen inches long and weighs about two pounds. Now the baby is nearly complete.

   With care, it could survive outside the womb—which could happen in the case of a premature birth. Naturally, it's better if it spends the following two months in the belly. Then it will be bigger and heavier and better prepared for life outside of the womb.

In the case of a premature birth, the baby must go into an incubator. There it will be warmed and sometimes artificially fed.

In the eighth month, walking around can be very strenuous for the mother. Often she suffers from back pains because the baby is now quite heavy. It weighs about five pounds and is just under eighteen inches long.

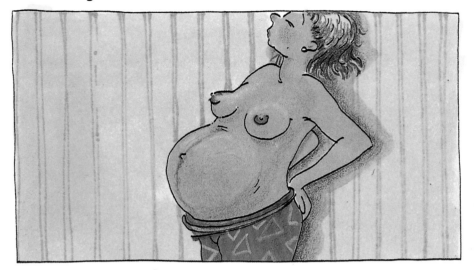

In the ninth month, most babies turn upside down in the uterus with their heads positioned toward the cervix. This is the ideal position for birth. The baby is now about eighteen inches long and weighs about six and a half pounds. At this point the uterus has been stretched so large that it reaches the mother's ribcage. Now the woman's body and the baby are ready for birth.

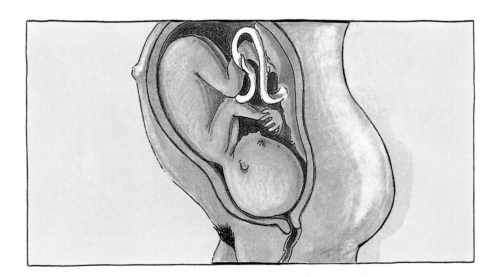

Shortly before birth, the baby is as heavy as a watermelon.

Nine and a half months after fertilization of the egg cell, the child enters the world. Sometimes the duration of the pregnancy is counted from the date of the last period, in which case it typically lasts ten months or exactly forty weeks.

A Baby Enters the World

It is Nearly Time

In the ninth month of pregnancy, the mother's distended belly sits very low on her torso. This is due to the uterus sinking downwards. The body is preparing itself for childbirth.

From now on, the woman must consider that her child could be born at any moment. Her regular check-ups with her gynecologist will need to become more frequent. At each appointment, the doctor uses a special apparatus called an **ultrasound scanner** to see how things look under the abdominal wall and in the woman's uterus.

Throughout the pregnancy, routine ultrasounds have helped the woman keep track of how her child is developing. But in the ninth month it is particularly important to make sure the baby has shifted positions, with its head is facing downward toward the cervix, as the baby must be born head first in order to avoid certain complications.

In addition, the gynecologist will check on the position of the baby's arms. At this stage, most will have them crossed over their chests. This enables the child to travel more easily through the **birth canal**, the passageway from the uterus through the cervix, vagina, and vulva.

If the baby has its back to the uterus opening, or is positioned feet-first (also called "breech"), then the birth will usually be very difficult. Sometimes the child can't pass through the birth canal without putting itself or the mother at risk. In these cases, the woman must give birth at a hospital, so that doctors can make an incision in her abdomen, and carefully deliver the baby from the uterus. This operation is called a **Cesarean section.**

If the child is positioned correctly in the womb, it is not required that a woman give birth in a hospital. If her doctor approves, the mother can also have the child at home. In that case, a **midwife** comes to the woman's home. Midwives are trained to assist mothers with their delivery, especially outside a hospital.

Some women might feel averse to giving birth in a hospital. However, if something goes wrong, the mother and child can typically receive better care at the hospital. Also, keep in mind that birth is very exhausting. At the hospital, the mother has time to recover and be taken care of while medical professionals help look after the baby.

The father is often present for the birth, either at home or at the hospital. He can assist by massaging his partner, holding her hand, wiping the sweat from her forehead, and comforting her through the pain. It can be very meaningful for the parents to experience the birth of their child together.

Birth is Very Exhausting

It is very difficult for a woman to give birth to a child. In fact, childbirth is often called "**labor**." Labor lasts an average of eight hours, but sometimes takes as long as eighteen hours! So it's no surprise that it takes a lot of strength and stamina to push the baby out.

As a woman's body prepares to go into labor, the mother will begin to notice **contractions**. These come from the uterus squeezing, or contracting, in order to push the baby through the birth canal, and feel similar to very severe abdominal pain. Contractions work like this: Imagine you're holding a wet bar of soap. If your hand is loose, nothing happens. But if you tighten your hand into a fist, the piece of soap slips out the side. Of course, the baby does not slip this easily out of the uterus. It can be a slow and painful process.

At first, the contractions come only rarely, then more and more frequently. When the contractions come regularly every five to ten minutes, this means the woman's body is going into labor: At this point the baby will have moved further down into the womb, bursting the amniotic sac. The contractions increase in frequency and intensity. Then the cervix opens. Both the cervix and the vagina can stretch very wide—like a balloon—to allow the baby to pass. Additionally, the baby's head and bones are still very soft, which helps it to slip out without being crushed.

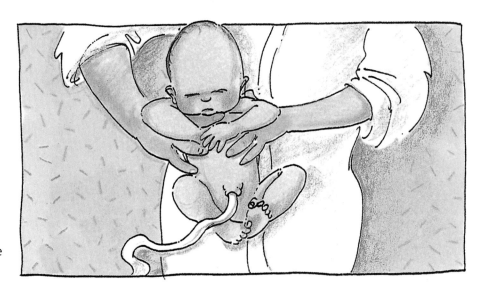

After the birth, the baby no longer needs the umbilical cord: It can breathe on its own and take in food

Everyone's Waiting for the First Cry

Finally, the baby's head can be seen in the vaginal opening. This is called "**crowning**." As soon as the baby is crowning, the doctor or midwife can reach in around the head and help to pull it out. Then comes the big moment. The baby begins to cry. This is the moment everyone has been waiting for: the mother, the father, the doctor, the midwife, and the nurse. The baby's first cry shows that the newborn person is alive and breathing on its own.

Once the baby has cried for the first time, it will be placed in its mother's arms as soon as possible. It's important for the baby to feel its mother's skin and heartbeat. Of course, it knows the latter one already from its time in the womb. Lying on the mother's chest usually has a calming effect on the baby.

After this little break, the doctor or midwife, or sometimes the father, cuts the umbilical cord. The baby no longer needs it, as it can now breathe on its own and take in food. Then the little boy or the little girl is bathed and wrapped in a soft cloth to keep it nice and warm. And finally, the baby can return to its mother.

This tiny person knows exactly what to do: It looks for the breast and begins to suckle milk. After just half an hour, the baby can already drink. It can also hear, smell, use its eyes to distinguish between light and dark.

The baby will remain in the hospital with its mother for about a week, during which both can rest and be checked on regularly. At this time, the mother might also get a few tips from the nurses on how to properly hold and care for such a small child. If you have never done it before, it is not so easy. At first, whenever the baby isn't with its mother, it rests inside an incubator. Here the baby has it almost as good as when it was in the womb. As soon as it is strong enough, it is allowed out of the incubator. A few days later it can leave the hospital with its mother.

Finally, the newborn sees, for the first time, the house or apartment where it will live.

The Littlest One Gets the Biggest Reception

People tend to get really excited when the baby is brought back from the hospital. The grandparents, the friends, uncles and aunts, the neighbors—they all want to meet the baby right away. Of course, they also ask how the mother is doing. But almost no one is interested in the baby's older siblings or the father.

Sometimes all the fuss over the baby can really get on the older siblings' nerves. When everything seems to revolve around the baby, a sibling can feel superfluous. Perhaps you have had a similar experience being the older sibling before. It can lead to a lot of bitterness.

But it usually doesn't take long for that initial curiosity and excitement to fade. Eventually your extended family and social circle will take an interest in people other than the baby again.

However, things at home will be different for a long time. Above all, your mother will have less time for you. She'll need to take care of the baby almost constantly. Sometimes, an older sibling will even feel jealous of the bond between their mother and the new baby, for example, when they see the new baby breast-feeding or napping in their mother's arms.

Now You're the "Big One"

Even if it feels to older siblings like their mother loves them less after welcoming a new baby, it's not true. Mothers always love their children.

And when it comes to how much they love them, there's no difference between older and younger children.

Remember, the baby is not the only special person in your family. You are, too. (And you also had your own big reception after being born!) Furthermore, when a younger sibling arrives, you get to take on the role of "big" sister or brother—and that's not bad at all.

Resources for Parents, Preteens, and Teens

Administration for Children and Families
U.S. Department of Health & Human Services
330 C Street SW
Washington, DC 20201
www.acf.hhs.gov

Advocates for Youth
Advocates for Youth
1325 G Street NW, Suite 980
Washington, DC 20005
www.advocatesforyouth.org

Amaze.org
AMAZE.org
c/o Advocates for Youth
1325 G Street NW, Suite 980
Washington, DC 20005
www.amaze.org

American Academy of Pediatrics (AAP)
American Academy of Pediatrics
National Headquarters
345 Park Boulevard
Itasca, IL 60143
www.aap.org

American Red Cross
American Red Cross National Headquarters
431 18th Street NW
Washington, DC 20006
www.redcross.org

American Sexual Health Association (ASHA)
ASHA
P.O. Box 13287
Research Triangle Park, NC 22709
www.ashasexualhealth.org

Centers for Disease Control and Prevention (CDC)
Centers for Disease Control and Prevention
1600 Clifton Road
Atlanta, GA 30333
www.cdc.gov

Head Start
U.S. Department of Health & Human Services
330 C Street SW
Washington, DC 20201
www.acf.hhs.gov/ohs

HealthyChildren.org
American Academy of Pediatrics
National Headquarters
345 Park Boulevard
Itasca, IL 60143
www.healthychildren.org

National Association for Family Child Care (NAFCC)
NAFCC
1743 West Alexander Street #201
Salt Lake City, UT 84119
www.nafcc.org

National Association for the Education of Young Children
NAEYC Headquarters
1313 L Street NW, Suite 500
Washington, DC 20005-4101
www.naeyc.org

National Center for Families Learning

National Center for Families Learning
325 W Main Street #300
Louisville, KY 40202
www.familieslearning.org

National Center for Parent, Family, and Community Engagement

U.S. Department of Health & Human Services
330 C Street SW
Washington, DC 20201
childcareta.acf.hhs.gov

National Institutes of Health (NIH)

National Institutes of Health
9000 Rockville Pike
Bethesda, MD 20892
www.nih.gov

Parents as Teachers

Parents as Teachers National Center, Inc.
2228 Ball Drive
St. Louis, MO 63146
www.parentsasteachers.org

Planned Parenthood

Planned Parenthood Federation of America
123 William Street, 10th Floor
New York, NY 10038
www.plannedparenthood.org

Unhushed

Unhushed
P.O. Box 92033
Austin, TX 78709
www.unhushed.org

Index